# CROSS CONNECTION

## AUTHOR'S EDITION

# MARK ROCHA

2nd Edition, 2022

This edition is published by Kindle Direct Publishing



Front cover photograph courtesy of Unsplash by Peteris Gertners, edited by Shashank Parab Illustration on page 27 by Flaticon.com

Cover design and typesetting by Mark Rocha

ISBN 9798839133808

# Index

# Index

# Preface

I was born and raised Catholic. But really, it doesn't matter what religion you were born into, I believe that it is safe to say that just like your name, it is one of those things that was chosen for you by someone else, most likely your parents. It wasn't a divine choice like your gender, height, ability, disability, or even the colour of your skin, eyes, or hair - it was a choice made by those who were co-responsible for your existence on this earth.

But here's the thing about choice, or free will. What sets us apart from other animals who operate on instinct, is also divine providence. So if free will is a divine gift, are we not allowed, by that same divinity, to accept, deny, approve, disprove, or go as far as to rename its existence? If you are bound strictly by faith, you may disagree, but you may feel differently if you stepped back for a moment. After all, our forefathers and ancestors did the same, when they 'chose' to create their Gods out of clay by looking up at the sky and marvelling at the sun, the moon, and the rain, or down at the earth and the fruit that it bore. There were those who 'chose' to create their Gods by writing books that told fantastical stories of men or women that flew, controlled the seas and oceans, manipulated lightning ... and even walked on water.

I was born and raised Catholic, but after many a Sunday school class, I started to ask questions that could not be answered. In today's information age, it's easy to read every religious text, revel in every

•••

story, and analyse every dogma - but it still does not answer one fundamental question - why. Why does this 'God' do what he or she does? Why did God choose me to exist on this earth? He willed me into existence with the help of my co-creators because he loves me, but if that's the case, why does he love me so much that he gave me amazing parents who have never left me wanting, provided me with a rich education, taken care of all my needs; yet abandoned countless others in desolation and despair, driven to delinquency, crime, or death? Why has he given me the ability and talent to write, sing, to create, yet taken away the function of my kidneys so that the remainder of my life becomes an even deeper mystery? Why? There are countless 'whys' that no one has the answer to.

If you ask any religious elder, they will say one thing, and one thing only - God has a plan, and I agree. If we who are made in his image and likeness can 'create' what we want with a plan in mind, so does this God. Yes, there's a plan, but why do we not know this plan? Is it not ironic that we are put on this planet and given the right to choose our journey, but not our destination? Because after all, we may feel that we are in control of or have the ability to control the instances in our lives - what to study, where to work, what to drive, who to marry. But once this journey has started, there is one thing that we cannot choose if we are willing to adhere to this plan, and that is how it ends.

•••

For the past couple of decades, I have wrestled with all these questions. And because this divine entity chose to give me the ability to think freely, I chose to question. And because I chose to question, I chose to write. I don't have the answers so you won't find them here. But what I do have is an opportunity to make you question as well. I was born Catholic, and though I may not be religious though I was raised to be, I am spiritual. I believe in divinity and purpose, that there is a force that is greater than all of us. What I do not believe, however, is that we have to choose just one. Because if I was not given the choice, then how can I?

You argue and you bicker, and you fight.
Atheists and Catholics,
Jews and Hindus argue day and night.
Over what they think is true.
But no one entertains the thought
that maybe God does not believe in you.

*From God's Perspective – Bo Burnham*

# If You Met God

If you met God today
What would you say?
What might he look like?
What might He say?

Would you tell him you're sorry
For the things you've done?
For the people you've cheated?
For the lies you've spun?

Or would you just stare
And say nothing at all?
Scared that at last
The wicked would fall?

Or maybe you'd explain
The cause of your plan,
And fail to remember
The one who made man.

Travelling continuously, no stop no
rest,
Priority cargo; must be delivered.
It took nine minutes to create man,
Nine months to create his saviour.

City limits, place to rest
Place to spend the restless night.
City limits, no place to rest
No place to spend the restless night.

All spaces filled, all but one;
Humbled by the stable behind.
Something is better than nothing,
Shelter in this house of meat.

The night is cold, unforgiving,
Waiting for the birth of forgiveness.
The hour of deliverance is at hand.
The hour of deliverance has come.

Great pain is taken upon herself,
A pain to end all pain.
Loves labour, the labour of love.
Alas, only cattle may witness this
joyous event.

Brought into the world on a bed of hay,
The radiance of a child in this dark
place.
No noise, no sound; quiet acceptance.
A loud silence is filled with song.

The heavens open up to see its work,
Choirs of angels sing his praise;
Deliverance has come, his name is
Emmanuel,
*Gloria, in excelsis deo.*

# Flower of Purity

Standing single and solemn
In a garden of prejudice and lust,
Was a beautiful flower;
Humble and filled with love.
The stench of the surroundings,
Of hatred and injustice,
Weighed heavy on the flower;
Yet it smelt of purity and sensitivity.
In the bleakness of this grey expanse,
Dark with lies and oppression;
This flower was a light,
White with innocence and joy.
This flower, however, grew and died;
But it died to give rise to a garden of
beauty.

## I Am ...

I am your neighbour, I am your friend,
I deliver your pizza, I live round the
bend.
I am your classmate, I am the nerd,
I eat in the canteen, I rescued a bird.
I am your doctor, I am your bro,
I clear your cheques, I open your door.
I work at your office, I beg on your
street,
I travel on buses, I prepare your meat.
I am your teacher, I play the guitar,
I wear blue jeans, I borrow your car.
You see me everywhere, you think I'm
a fraud,
Yet I am in everything, for I am ... your
God.

# At The Wall

Five men stood still with their backs to
a wall,
Opposite them stood another five.
Five were blindfolded to spare them the
sight,
Five to die and five to survive.
They all stood erect, their duty was
clear,
They all waited for the call;
And when it was done, five men stood–
While they watched the blindfolds fall.

Blessed are you who is giving
I have found my treasure in you

Blessed are you who is kind
I have felt the warmth of your heart

Blessed are you who is simple
I have seen the riches of this world

Blessed are you who is patient and
understanding
I have found the way to my soul

Blessed are you for forgiving
I have been cleansed of the errors I
have made

Blessed are you who is pure
I am bathed in the light of your love

Blessed are you who is miraculous
I rejoice in the wonder of you

Blessed are you who is mine
For now I inherit the world

Eight

# God of Our Fathers

'they also serve who only stand and
wait'
– *'On His Blindness' by John Milton*

***

Kneel before me, cover your head;
Take off your shoes.
Ashen your face, beat your breasts;
Mourn, repentance for your sins.
Heed commandments, fast, and pray;
Sacrifice burnt offerings – dead
animals.
Rest one day, work six.
Die, acceptance of your life.

## Empty

Now I lay me down to sleep,
But in my head, I howl and weep.
Tears, like the rain they fall;
Tears, bitter as the gall.
I try to hide the pain, but still
I am hurt against my will.
If I should die before I wake,
What good is there for me to take?
My heart is blacker than the night,
My heart is shattered by the light.
Only God can save my soul,
Only God can fill this hole.

I need to feed of mortal pain,
A crown of thorns perhaps;
But sitting back on pews, aloof,
The lie becomes alive.

I do believe in existential
Idiosyncrasy,
But in death the world is clear,
The motive, still a dream.

You preach about eternal end,
I see beyond the door;
But who would walk the extra mile?
Whose house is not a home?

Like blood that washed the saviour's
face,
Like bitter herbs and wine;
The symbols are like Braille to blind,
Yet who's graduated life?

Close your eyes, relax, forget;
the hand is cold, the hand of death –
the pulse it fades, the music stops to
rest ...
you feel it now – damnation at its best.

Injected for the purpose of relief,
infliction of the pain you felt the least;
and down the hall the swinging doors
have closed –
your bleeding heart to feast on, lies
exposed.

The lights, the sordid colour of the
walls;
in blues and greens, as silently the red
falls
to cover the stain you left upon your
life –
brought forth by careful placement of
the knife.

Fight hard the losing battle for the sake
of life – that soon you may consciously
awake ...
your story has been written before your
time,
the music stopped, but the words in
line.

She weeps on the side not knowing
why,
she longs for the reason, "why did you
make me cry?"
he can hear her, but he cannot explain;
so he peers through the dark, as she
steers through the pain.

"End it now, make it stop, take it all;
it must go, take my hand, let me fall;
for the sin of this life is my own ...
what we started let me finish alone."

From pillar to post he did run,
begging, pleading, not praying to the
one;
knowing too well that his tongue had
been cut,
and the doors in the sky had been shut.

Close your eyes, in the darkness reflect,
as you cling to the fingers of death –
what was given to you, you did sell,
now your life has no story to tell.

# The Truth

Don't speak to me in ignorance,
You don't know how I feel.
You think you know me inside out,
But you're further than the real.
You're selfish in your attitude,
You never spare a thought;
To think about the others,
Who have given you what you've got.
You'll never know just how it feels,
To gain the love or trust;
Of that person who is special,
Lying buried in the dust.

his silver skin, lac'd with his golden
blood
- *Macbeth, William Shakespeare*

***

So convinced was he that the deed to be
done
Was the deed to be done,
And the need to become accursed by
the One
Was indeed to be done upon him and
his son
Though he had not one.

And so he was sent to the room where
he lay
With a dagger in hand so that he could
slay
Before the break of day,
The man who though grey, was sent by
God
To rule in His way –

But dammed be the man who now
cannot pray,
Who cannot say 'Amen' again to this
day.

The deed is complete, the murder was
sweet;
The host and the hostess can now go to
sleep.
But in sleep do they weep, and seek a
fate bleak;
For dammed will they be, 'cause their
soul they can't keep.

# An Ode of Thanks

No one could understand me
at all like she did;
talk to me, make me laugh.
Anytime I needed someone,
she was there, ready to
help me with my problems.

Ask and you shall receive, and so I
asked – and so generous was the
Father, that he manifested himself in
her to make me
feel like the only
one in the world.

So every night I thank God for her, the
only person who makes me feel
complete.

# Our God

as god on high
lets babies cry
and evil men to lie
no yours no my
a price too high
all beings with life
must die

# Forsaken Crop

There's anger growing in my mind,
a cure for which I cannot find.
It eats away my tender skin,
the power of the seventh sin.
I hold it in release it not,
my body begins to rot;
The juices boil inside my spleen,
I see a place I have not seen.
Can't hold it back, I self explode;
I have released a heavy load.
I look around to see my deed,
My anger was a deadly seed.

He remains unclean as long as he has
the disease,
And must live outside the camp, away
from others.
*– Lev 13:46*

***

From whence comes this swelling,
This unwelcome, unannounced guest?
Maybe today and gone tomorrow?
But to the elder I must go,
He shall examine it and make his
diagnosis.
For six days I am isolated – come the
seventh I am checked.
The swelling's increased, its being
spread – dreaded skin disease.
Damned am I, accursed be the one who
looks on me.
No longer do I belong to my people,
Thrown out to suffer alone.
Clothes torn and hair uncut.
But who are you who approach me?
I cover my lower lip and cry 'unclean,
unclean' You hear and still you
approach.
Poorer than poor, yet much richer;
One of wealth – though you have none.
Only one thing you can give me – and
so I beg thee,
'Please sir, if you want – heal me ...'

# Come Down

*It states plainly,*
*The laws of physics apply –*
*Anything that goes up*
*Must come down.*

I increased my trust in you,
    Now it must come down.
I increased my faith in you,
    Now it must come down.
I raise this knife above you,
    Now it must come down.
You once were raised to life,
But now ... you must come down.

Conclusion

Accept me for who I am
Not for how I appear.
Do not judge me,
By listening to what I say.
Who are you,
That you should analyze?
Who are you,
That you should compare?
Reason without practicality,
Logic without learning;
Choices without opinion,
Conclusions based on assumptions.

# Holy Man

Holy man I come to you
For answers to my prayers;
Show me what I'm seeking,
Show me the hidden stairs.

Holy man I ask of you
To look into my past;
Tell me what went wrong there,
Tell me what I ask.

Holy man I beg of you
Please tell me what's to come;
Will I be successful?
Will I meet that special one?

Oh Holy man please look at me
And help me to decide
The path I have to take,
To reach the other side.

# My Life

I've been living a lie
The person I am;
The things that I want,
The ground where I stand.
I'm living stagnated
Denied and alone;
I'm sleeping awake,
On sand, not stone.

The question of my mortality weighs
heavy on my heart,
The answer to it hangs heavier over my
head.
Time grows longer, as it becomes
shorter;
I leave here so that I may come to you.

*Eli Eli, lama sabachtani?*

All my friends have deserted me,
Neither blood nor water do I have;
All I have is you,
Yet right now, you seem the furthest
away.

*Eli Eli, lama sabachtani?*

In all my life, never once have I
doubted you;
Never have I craved independence.
But now I'm alone, independent
against my will;
You can exist without me,
I can't exist without you.

*Eli Eli, lama sabachtani?*

Forsaken

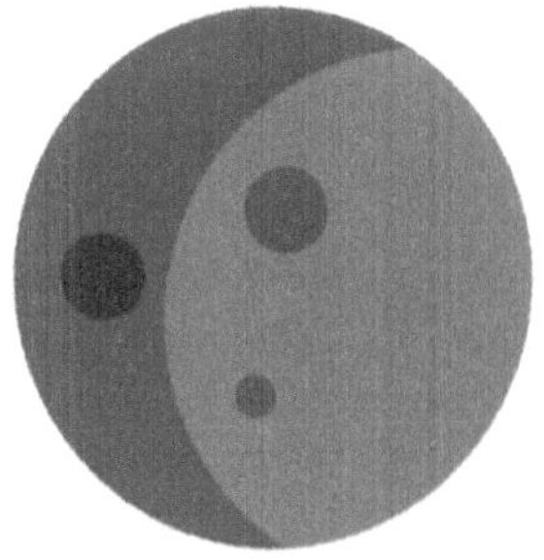

# Yellow Moon

Yellow moon just like the sun,
Chasing feathers on the run.
Yellow like a summer ray,
Beckons for a rainy day.
Why you're painted no one knows,
Nestled in the sky you glow;
Yellow moon so pale you are,
Close to me, but yet so far.

In Coma

She opened her eyes today
They said she wouldn't
          They were wrong.
She sat up and asked for water
There wasn't any there.
She closed her eyes again
They knew she would
          It was expected
Frigid, she lay there lifeless
They didn't really care.

put me in a beaker
fill it with water
seal out the air
drown my body
redeem my soul

what do you want from me?
why am I an object of contempt?
is there a flaw in your creation?
is there correction in the creator?

the trial by fire is not purification
the trial by fire is pain
the trial by fire will not help you
the trial by fire is in vain

love me for who I am
love me for what I do
don't play me as a hand
for no good comes from the things you
do

visions in my semi-conscious state
curdle my blood, render me cold.
there's no hope for those who come
after me
all must die – who do not believe

the time of action is here
the time of action is now
don't ask questions, you'll get no
answers
the bible tells you how

seep into my mind, tear my brain in
half;
seep into my mind, despair thy evil
laugh.

# Responsible of Guilt

How grave were my actions toward
you;
That bitterness should flow from you
like rivers?

From the depths of your heart
drenched in hatred;
From your mind blinded by the dark.

There's no room for reason and
discernment;
There's no scope for forgiveness or
love.

Your body is blemished by your own
blood;
Your soul, scarred by your guilt.

# Number of the Beast

The number is on your forehead
it's written in your palm;
I read it in the ending,
It started with a psalm.
May those with wisdom see it,
may mathematicians count;
let he who knows reveals what spawns
from the fiery fount.

Seven

Lazy, I lie in want, not begotten.
Greed eats me; I give in – that which is
not mine.
I have, you don't, I think you want.
One more thing still to achieve – bodily
desire.
You have, I don't, I know I want.
I can't achieve, I grind my teeth;
I grind your bones, I take my leave.
Seven ways to break ten
commandments.

# Inveigh

Deaf ears lie open for you to abuse;
For you to point fingers,
For you to accuse.
Clenched fists hang ready for you to
employ;
For you to be flagrant,
For you to enjoy.
Blue eyes close softly for you to accept;
For tears to fall freely,
For you to regret.
Stone hearts lie lifeless for you to
ignore;
To rule without reason,
To show them the door.

## Drug

All I have is now,
now is where it ends;
an end to sum it all,
what started first as friends.
But soon grew into love,
a love that fell too fast;
an outline of who we were,
now hidden in the past.

# The All-Knowing

Don't listen to them – them who are right
Them who appear without sin;
Though the mistakes they made are buried in time,
You will find their errors within.

Don't listen to them – them who are smart
Them who think that they know;
Though the good that they've done is thrown in your face,
You will find that that good will not grow.

Listen to yourself – you who are true
You who knows what is right;
The decisions you make will be yours till the end
When it's you left alone in your fight.

Death – Life – Death

I open my eyes, and it's dark.
I try to move myself,
But am confined by walls.
I reach up, solid ceiling.

Where am I?
One minute I'm driving my car,
The next minute I'm on my back
Struggling to get out.

It's getting stuffy.
I can barely breathe.
I realize where I am and panic.
I scrape at the ceiling with madness.

With wood chips in my nails,
I lash out violently at the walls.
As I tire my self, I realise that I've used
up all the oxygen.
I'm weak, I can't see, my lungs close,
I'm...

Six feet above, a priest signs himself
and says:
"Eternal rest give unto his soul O Lord
And let perpetual light shine upon him.
May his soul rest in peace. Amen"

# Templar

I worked hard to reach here,
Now nothing can stand in my way.
I fought hard the battles,
And struggled night and day.
I moved onwards not back
And never questioned my goal;
I sacrificed and killed,
For the redemption of my soul.

Like face of make up made up,
Like book who hath a cover lied;
We crawl inside our little selves,
Too small to show, too big to hide.
We know too much, they know not we,
We know what we cans't know;
And for fear of being brought into the
light,
We hide and force our guilt to grow.
But time can only last so long,
As time shall fill the time;
And soon the hour shall don on us,
An hour when the sun shall shine.
And oh what sorrow, oh what pain;
Our guilty conscience plays,
And 'never shall sun that morrow see',
Never, to the end of days.

Unknown

# Cross Connection

Stripped naked, he's thrown on the
bark.
His hands are gaping,
Belching blood incarnadine.
His feet are mirrored images,
Pinned down to prevent escape;
The result of persistent banging on a
metal shaft.
With a pierced crown,
He cries to the Lord for help which he
knows he will not receive.
He gives up and bows his head.
The carpenter, killed by his profession.

The tree was planted firmly
And accompanied by two;
The three all hung together
In the middle was the Jew.

All had a crime committed
But none of them the same;
One had robbed, another killed,
Another said his name.

They had a common father,
Two would soon return;
One would then come back again,
For the other did not learn.

And by the double flowing stream,
Where lepers healed their sores;
A branch hung low of heavy load,
While silver closed the doors.

*In Memoriam*

# Ocean's Embrace

Standing on the water's edge
    He called you from afar,
to be a zephyr in the day –
    at night to be a star.
No one willed you leave us,
    no one willed you go;
but still you went to be with Him
    and be with us no more.
You didn't go by way of man,
    no needle, rope or knife;
He bid you come through Baptism –
    through that which gave you
life.
And now our home is empty,
    our lives emptier still;
all because He called
    And you surrendered to His will.

# One Last Photograph

This camera has seen its fair share of
negatives
Changing subjects, some still, shooting
snapshots ahead of this
Constantly moving, one frame,
twenty-four of it
Colours combine bringing life where
there wasn't it

No moment was stagnant, you stood on
the precipice
You looked down and saw the whole
world through your mirrorless
Clicked every second, the past had your
hands in it
Memories painted from birth to a
wedding dress

Taking us back to a time been before
Your one eye closed, with your heart
keeping score
Not knowing what that half-open
shutter would store
But now this album can't hold any
more

These celluloid portraits will forever be
true
A reminder that life's fleeting
moments are few
So if there was just one more thing I
could do
I would take one last photograph - a
picture of you

*When doubt creates mountains*

*Faith moves them*